Th

Swami Pavitrananda

Advaita Ashrama
(PUBLICATION DEPARTMENT)
5 DEHI ENTALLY ROAD · KOLKATA 700 014

Published by
Swami Tattwavidananda
Adhyaksha, Advaita Ashrama
Mayavati, Champawat, Uttarakhand, Himalayas
from its Publication Department, Kolkata
Email: mail@advaitaashrama.org
Website: www.advaitaashrama.org

ISBN 978-81-7505-031-0

Printed in India at
Trio Process
Kolkata 700 014

PREFACE

In the following pages will be found the story of a life which was lived so silently and unostentatiously that its very simplicity was bewildering. Yet the depth of its richness seemed unfathomable even to those who were universally respected for their spiritual greatness. Indeed such a life defies analysis, and it is much more difficult to portray it. We may not comprehend greatness as a whole, but still does not even a partial glimpse of it often bring us infinite good? Therein lies our justification for making the present attempt.

In preparing this work we have got considerable help from the following books: *Sri Ramakrishna Lilaprasanga, Mayer Katha*, Parts I & II, and *Sri Sarada Devi*. Of these the first two are in Bengali, published by the Udbodhan Office, Calcutta, and the last one is in English, published by the Ramakrishna Math, Madras.

Advaita Ashrama   PUBLISHER
Mayavati, Himalayas
September 2, 1942

Holy Mother Sri Sarada Devi

Beloved Mother,

This morning, early, I went to church—to pray for Sara. All the people there were thinking of Mary, the Mother of Jesus, and suddenly I thought of you. Your dear face, and your loving look and your white Sari and your bracelets. It was all there. And it seemed to me that yours was the Presence that was to soothe and bless poor S. Sara's sickroom. And—do you know?—I thought I had been very foolish to sit in your room, at the evening service to Sri Ramakrishna, trying to meditate. Why did I not understand that it was quite enough to be a little child at your dear feet? Dear Mother! You are full of love! And it is not a flushed and violent love, like ours, and like the world's, but a gentle peace that brings good to everyone and wishes ill to none. It is a golden radiance, full of play. What a blessed Sunday that was, a few months ago, when I ran in to you, the last thing before I went on the Ganges—ran back to you for a moment—as soon as I came back! I felt such a wonderful freedom in the blessing you gave me, and in your welcome home! Dearest

*Mother! I wish we could send you a wonderful hymn,
or a prayer. But somehow even that would seem too
loud, too full of noise! Surely you are the most wonderful thing of God—Sri Ramakrishna's own chalice
of His Love for the world—a token left with His children, in these lonely days, and we should be very still
and quiet before you—except indeed for a little fun!
Surely the 'wonderful things of God' are all quiet—
stealing unnoticed into our lives—the air and the sun-
light and the sweetness of gardens and of the Ganges.
These are the silent things that are like you!*

*Do send to poor S. Sara the mantle of your peace.
Isn't your thought, now and then, of the high calm
that neither loves nor hates? Isn't that a sweet bene-
diction that trembles in God, like the dewdrop on the
lotus-leaf, and touches not the world?*

*Ever, my darling Mother, your foolish KHOOKI
(baby),*

Nivedita

A LETTER BY SISTER NIVEDITA
TO THE HOLY MOTHER

CONTENTS

Holy Mother Sri Sarada Devi

I
THE DISCOVERY OF SARADAMANI

After Sri Ramakrishna had the first vision of the Divine Mother, he was consumed with a thirst to have it constantly. He was like a man who had once had access to an invaluable treasure, but which had again been closed to him. So he was burning with a desire to repeat that experience. His desire was so intense and his longing so severe that he could no longer behave like a normal man. Seeing his strange actions and behaviour many thought that he was out of his mind. The news reached his old mother, who was at their native village, Kamarpukur. She felt very anxious for her son and had him brought to her, so that by careful nursing she might cure him.

When Sri Ramakrishna came to Kamarpukur, his mother thought that marriage might bring down his mind to worldly things and he might be cured of his divine malady. So she sent emissaries here and there to negotiate with various persons but a suitable bride could not be found. Strangely enough, Sri Ramakrishna took a child-like interest in these proceedings; and finding his mother in a great predicament about his bride, he himself suggested that there was a little girl who might be suitable—the daughter of Ram Chandra Mukhopadhyaya—at Jayrambati, only six kilometers away.

His mother, Chandramani, took up this suggestion, sent a man to Jayrambati and learnt that the girl, beaming with divine effulgence, was not only the pet child of her parents and family but also the idol of the whole village. There was something in her which even at that early age drew everybody to her. Whoever saw this little girl could not but feel a fascination for her. So Chandra Devi at once agreed to have her as her daughter-in-law. The marriage was arranged and performed with Sri Ramakrishna's own consent, in spite of the fact that his thoughts constantly soared high above the earthly region.

The name of the bride, who was afterwards known as the Holy Mother to innumerable disciples and admirers of Sri Ramakrishna, was Saradamani. Her father, Ram Chandra Mukhopadhyaya, was a very pious Brahmin; her mother, Shyamasundari Devi, was also known for her great piety. Being very poor, Ram Chandra had to struggle very hard for his livelihood and the maintenance of the family. The income from his priestly duties was too meagre for his needs, so he had to supplement it by agricultural pursuits and the making of sacred threads. Nevertheless Ram Chandra was known for his kindness and generosity. He had a very tender heart which felt distress at the suffering of others. In 1864, when a terrible famine devastated Bengal and the little village of Jayrambati and the neighbourhood did not escape the ravages of the scourge, Ram Chandra would daily feed large a number of starving people out of his surplus produce of the previous year, without caring for his own diffi-cult circumstances. No wonder Ram Chandra was the object of great reverence and deep affection of the whole locality.

II
THE DARLING OF THE VILLAGE

Saradamani was born on 22 December 1853, about seventeen years after the birth of Sri Ramakrishna. Born in a poor family, though the darling of all, she had to do many of the hard household duties to help her parents. She was the eldest child, and she had to take care of her six younger brothers and sisters. She would take food to the servants in the fields, she would cut grass for the cows in neck-deep water, and she would collect grain from the fields in the paddy season. All these have a very touching interest when we know that afterwards in her advanced years she gave spiritual ministration to thousands of persons who would have been ready to spend literally everything to fulfil her slightest wish. But even in more favourable circumstances she lived the same simple life—liking her ordinary village dishes, doing the duties and following a routine of life similar to those of other women of that poor little village. Actually her life was more strenuous than theirs as her family was very exacting and also because many devotees would flock to her village home. But in her early age, when she would be going about in the fields and doing hard labour, though her presence would invariably light up joy in the surroundings, who did know that here was an almost divine being walking in their midst!

As a young girl, Saradamani was rather grave for her age. None would find in her any childish frivolity, and she had little interest in the games commonly played by children of her age. But she was the embodiment of innocence and simplicity, and her love for other children was compelling. That made her the natural mediator when there was any quarrel among other girls. She would prefer to play with the clay images of the deities Kali and Lakshmi rather than with ordinary dolls; and would worship them with great devotion with flowers and sacred leaves. She had a great aptitude for meditation. One day while the worship of the goddess Jagaddhatri was going on, she sat meditating on the Divine Mother with so much absorption that a bystander was struck with awe at the sight.

Saradamani had little formal education. Along with her younger brothers she would now and then go to school, but nobody took her education seriously. On the contrary, she sometimes met with positive discouragement. Later at Kamarpukur, when she was found reading a Bengali primer,

Hriday, a nephew of Sri Ramakrishna, snatched away the book saying that it would develop in her a tendency to read novels and dramas. But because of her own interest she later learnt in a general way to read books through the help of Lakshmi, a niece of Sri Ramakrishna, and also through another girl at Dakshineswar who would come to see her on her way to the Ganga for bathing. Afterwards the Holy Mother would read the Ramayana or similar books at leisure, but she was never found to write.

That does not mean, however, that the Holy Mother had no education in the real sense of the term. In her village home she had plenty of opportunities to see religious dramas and to listen to Pauranic stories, and she would attend many religious festivals. She was brought up under the influence of parents who were of the finest character. And above all, she had the rare privilege of coming into the closest contact with one who not only had the power to transform but actually did transform many lives by his silent and unconscious influence. As such the Holy Mother embodied the result of the best education. Her natural dignity, combined with motherly affection for one and all, her tender courtesy along with great broad-mindedness indicating the highest development of mind, compelled not only love and reverence, but at times wonder and awe.

III
MARRIAGE

Saradamani was very young, when she was married—so young that she could not clearly remember the event. She would afterwards say: 'I was married when the dates ripen. Within ten days of the marriage, when I went to Kamarpukur, I used to gather dates from under the trees.' Such a little girl married and Sri Ramakrishna giving consent to the marriage! To those who are very critical about it and pretend to be shocked, we may say that this kind of marriage is no more than a mere betrothal after which the girl usually returns to her parents until sufficiently grown up. And in this particular case, the bridegroom lived on such a high plane that he could give no more serious thought to the marriage than a little boy gives to his playthings.

This time Sri Ramakrishna stayed at Kamarpukur a little over two years. Before he returned to Dakshineswar he paid a short visit to his father-in-law's house in obedience to the family custom, and brought Saradamani back to Kamarpukur with him for a few days. At this time

Saradamani was only seven—her mind not yet sufficiently developed even to know what marriage was.

When Sri Ramakrishna returned to Dakshineswar, divine longing again seized him in all its intensity, and he forgot all about Kamarpukur, his friends and relations, and everything. The one thought which occupied his whole mind was how to realize the Divine Mother as a constant presence. A severe spiritual storm seized him. Days and nights were spent in anguish because God was not a living reality to him: if the Divine Mother was a reality why should She not be to him as tangible as the visible objects around? He was consumed with that one longing. Sleep left him, he forgot all idea of food and drink. Worldly things or any talk about worldly affairs he dreaded and shunned as poison.

While he was passing through this state of divine discontent, smaller minds thought that he was seized with a disease, that his brain was deranged. Physicians were called in, medicines were tried, but all to no avail. The news gradually travelled to Kamarpukur that Sri Ramakrishna had gone mad. Chandramani was anxious for her beloved son. She began to pray for him and offered worship to various gods. Jayrambati being so near to Kamarpukur, the news certainly reached Jayrambati too. But his wife being so young was perhaps unconcerned about the happenings at Dakshineswar.

Saradamani's two subsequent visits to Kamarpukur were at the ages of thirteen and fourteen years, when both Sri Ramakrishna and his mother were at Dakshineswar. The next time she went there, in 1867, she was privileged to stay with Sri Ramakrishna. When he arrived at Kamarpukur in that year, his anxious relatives and friends found that with all his deep religious feeling he was quite a normal man in his ordinary dealings. That was a great relief to them. At this time Saradamani was brought to Kamarpukur from her father's house. This might be, in a sense, her first meeting with her husband.

Sri Ramakrishna lived at Kamarpukur for about seven months. During this stay he did one great thing. Though his mind would constantly soar to the transcendental level so that he was generally indifferent to anything worldly, when Saradamani came to Kamarpukur he seriously set about giving her proper training. Sri Ramakrishna was by now a sannyasin.[1] When his guru, Totapuri, learnt that he had married, he remarked: 'What if you are married! The real test

---

1. A person who has formally renounced the world, a monk.

of love for God is that even if the wife be near,
the mind will not gravitate to the thought of
sense-pleasure. If one knows that all is Brahman,
what difference can one make between one sex
and another? One is above all these ideas.' These
significant words of the Guru came to be illus-
trated in the case of the disciple, as Sri Ramakrishna now met Saradamani and turned his
mind to the fulfillment of his educational duties
to his wife.

Whatever Sri Ramakrishna would do, he
would always do with perfect thoroughness. So
when he took upon himself the task of training
Saradamani, he brought to bear upon the work a
sense of completeness. He talked to her not only
of high spiritual matters but also taught her how
to do ordinary household duties. Saradamani,
pure as purity itself, brought up in the innocent
and unsophisticated atmosphere of village life,
and unsullied by any worldly thought, found in
Sri Ramakrishna not a husband in the common
sense of the term but one who was the embodiment of unspeakable love. Of her experiences of
this period she used to say afterwards: 'I felt as if
a vessel full of divine bliss was permanently
installed in my heart. I cannot adequately describe
the heavenly joy which filled my heart.' She
obviously felt that she had the rare privilege of
receiving an unearthly treasure.

With such feelings she went back to
Jayrambati when Sri Ramakrishna again returned
to Dakshineswar. After Sri Ramakrishna reached
Dakshineswar, to all intents and purposes, he
again forgot all about Saradamani. But it was different with his wife, who had received such
unalloyed bliss from him. Her constant thought
was centered on him. She longed to be with him
at Dakshineswar. But she consoled herself with
the thought that one who had shown her such
tender consideration at the very first meeting
could not have forgotten her altogether. There
would certainly come a time when she would be
called to his side. Patiently and silently she waited
for that auspicious moment.

IV
FIRST VISIT TO DAKSHINESWAR

At this period one could find a decided change in her conduct and behaviour. She now became more quiet and serious, an embodiment of love and sympathy for all, and ready to adapt herself to any circumstance. Her inward bliss was so great that no earthly difficulty or suffering could affect her. She would have continued in that exalted state except for the fact that whispers went round in that small village that her husband had gone mad. While Sri Ramakrishna passed his days in divine ecstasy, people interpreted his extra-ordinary behaviour as signs of mental derangement. And this news spread to all his relations. People of Jayrambati began to show sympathy for Saradamani's sad plight , little knowing that the expression of such sympathy made her suffering much worse. Saradamani avoided socializing and busied herself with work, so that she might not have to hear any gossip with reference to her husband. But the rumour was very strong that Sri Ramakrishna had gone mad, that he went about naked and muttered unintelligible words.

'Could it be true?' thought Saradamani to herself, 'Is he then not what I found him to be? If it be so, then it is my duty to be by him at this critical moment.' But how could she go to Dakshineswar? The idea was next to impossible for a person like her—situated as Jayrambati was at such a great distance and the communication also so difficult.

But the silent prayers of a sincere and devoted heart were heard by God and an unexpected opportunity presented itself to Saradamani for going to Dakshineswar. On an auspicious occasion, some women from neighbouring villages were going to Calcutta for a bath in the Ganga. Saradamani expressed a desire to be in that pilgrim party. When the news reached the ears of her father, he at once understood the real cause behind her desire. So he readily gave permission and himself accompanied the party so that his beloved Sarada might be well taken care of. The distance of about a hundred kilometers had to be covered on foot. Only the rich could afford to go in a palanquin.[1] As that luxury was out of the question for poor Ram Chandra, he along with his daughter started on foot. Saradamani, unaccustomed to walking a long distance, found the journey strenuous. But physical suffering was

---

[1] A type of carriage borne on the shoulders of bearers.

nothing compared to the joy of meeting the Master. So she altogether ignored any hardship that came on the way. But on the third day, before the party could reach Calcutta, Saradamani had a high fever. It was impossible for her to walk in spite of her desire to continue the journey. So a shelter had to be found in a cottage built for travellers. At night the fever rose very high, and Saradamani lost all outward consciousness. The Holy Mother used to narrate afterwards that while she was in that condition she saw in a vision that a girl dark in complexion but exquisitely beautiful in appearance sat by her side caressing and nursing her. When asked who she was, the girl said that she came from Dakshineswar, that she was the Holy Mother's sister and had come all the way to receive her. After that Saradamani fell asleep. Strange to say, the next morning the fever was gone, and she was able to start. On the way she had fever again, but Ram Chandra somehow managed to reach Dakshineswar by nightfall.

What was the anxiety of Sri Ramakrishna to see Saradamani come in that condition! Immediately he busied himself in making all arrangements for the patient and set up a bed for her in his own room. Often he repeated in great sorrow, but with childlike simplicity: 'You have come when dear Mathur is no more. Had he been alive, no difficulty whatsoever would arise as to taking care of you. Now that he is gone, who can take his place?' But did Saradamani receive less care? Sri Ramakrishna himself began to nurse and attend to her day and night, and that so carefully that in the course of three or four days she was all right. After that Saradamani was shifted to the ground floor of the Nahabat,[1] where she stayed with Chandramani, her mother-in-law, who was at that time at Dakshineswar.

Saradamani could hardly believe her eyes when she found her husband, who was reported to have gone mad, feeling so much anxiety at her illness and showing so much kindness and affection. Was there any woman in this world so blessed as to receive such loving care from her husband? Saradamani knew for certain that whatever might be people's opinion, her divine husband was perfectly sane; not only that, but there had not been the least change in his attitude toward her.

Ram Chandra was glad to see his daughter happy and comfortable at Dakshineswar. So he returned to his village home, leaving Saradamani in the privileged position of serving her husband

---

[1] A very small two-storeyed building, close to Sri Ramakrishna's room, the upper storey of which was intended for temple music.

and old mother-in-law. It was in March of 1872 that the Holy Mother reached Dakshineswar—about five years after she had last seen the Master at Kamarpukur.

Sri Ramakrishna at this time lived in constant divine communion. The greater part of the day and night he would remain in an ecstatic condition. Even a slight incident—the singing of a devotional song or the sight of anything which had a divine association, however remote—would throw his mind into samadhi, and he would become oblivious of his surroundings. He was more at home on the divine plane than we are on the earthly plane. But when Saradamani arrived at Dakshineswar he was not forgetful of his duties to his wedded wife. If she so desired, Sri Ramakrishna was willing to sacrifice his very mission for her. Saradamani also, on her part, was too pure and noble to have the slightest inclination to drag her saintly husband to a life of worldliness. She clearly told him about this and readily responded to his ideals and aspirations. All that she wanted was to be near him and to have the privilege of serving him and moulding her own life according to his direction. Sri Ramakrishna gave her that favour in abundance. Though the Holy Mother was accommodated at the Nahabat and in the course of the day could not meet the Master because he had visitors, at night she was allowed to stay in his room and share the same bed with him. Saradamani at this time would receive from her divine husband instructions in high spiritual matters as well as about mundane things. It was not a life of conjugal relations but of great spiritual training—so much so that the wife in Saradamani was merged in the disciple in her. Afterwards nobody could perceive in her utterances and behaviour anything that betrayed her special claim on Sri Ramakrishna. She was only the humble disciple of the Master, and this was to her a matter of supreme joy and privilege.

V
RELATIONSHIP WITH THE MASTER

And what was the attitude of Sri Ramakrishna towards her? Never for a moment did he look upon her as a wife, except for the fact that he owned a duty to her as regards her training in matters spiritual as well as earthly. His consciousness regarding Saradamani swung between anxious solicitude for one who needed care, and great reverence for one who was the embodiment of the Divine Mother. Though he would give her earnest instructions in all matters, with what reverence did he look upon her! 'My very devotion to God will take wings, if her feelings are even slightly hurt,' Sri Ramakrishna used to say. 'How do you look upon me?' Saradamani once asked Sri Ramakrishna as she was serving him massaging his feet. 'The same Divine Mother who is staying at the temple is now massaging me,' came the prompt reply from Sri Ramakrishna. To him there was no difference between Saradamani and the Deity in the Kali temple.

But this was not the outcome of mere religious sentimentalism—an artificial attempt to look upon all women as the embodiment of the Blissful Mother. Everything Sri Ramakrishna said or believed was the result of his personal experience, and he was always bold in his experimentation—sometimes dangerously bold. Did he see in the Image in the temple a living presence? Well, he must know for certain whether his vision was a fact or a hallucination. He placed a piece of cotton under the nostrils of the Image just to test whether there was any indication of life. Thus the simplicity of a child and the courage of a scientist were combined in him. With the same boldness and simplicity Sri Ramakrishna asked himself one day whether he had really forgotten the wife in Saradamani or whether there lurked any carnal desire in him. Saradamani was by his side in the same bed. But before he could think of any physical relationship with her, his mind was thrown into deep samadhi and his body-consciousness was absolutely gone. And in that state he passed the rest of the night.

'The credit for this was no less due to her,' Sri Ramakrishna used to remark afterwards. Saradamani's snow-white purity was his shield and armour. Sri Ramakrishna once prayed to the Divine Mother after his marriage that any least trace of carnal desire might be removed from the mind of his wife. Sri Ramakrishna would say in later times, 'When I lived with her (meaning

Saradamani) from day to day at this period, I understood that the Divine Mother had really heard my prayer.'

One thing which Sri Ramakrishna greatly emphasized was the need of harmony between one's words and deeds, and this dictum expressed itself in every breath of his life. How literally Sri Ramakrishna looked upon Saradamani as the manifestation of the Divine Mother in the flesh can be judged from the following incident which happened one night at Dakshineswar during this time. It was a special day in the month of May for the worship of the Divine Mother. The temple of Dakshineswar wore an air of festivity. Everybody was busy with the worship that would be performed at night. Sri Ramakrishna expressed a desire to have personal worship of the Mother in his own room, and all arrangements were made for this. Twilight passed into evening, and the darkness of the new-moon night enveloped the surroundings. At the end of the first watch of the night Sri Ramakrishna sat for the worship. The seat where the Deity was to be installed was in front of him. He performed the preliminaries of the worship. Saradamani had previously been instructed to come and attend the worship. She came and was watching the whole thing. The spiritual atmosphere which was created by Sri Ramakrishna's intense devotion made

Saradamani oblivious of the outside world and she had already entered a mood of partial ecstasy. As he proceeded with the worship, Sri Ramakrishna beckoned to her to sit on the seat arranged for the Deity. In that semiconscious state, not knowing what she was doing, Saradamani took the seat reserved for the Mother. Sri Ramakrishna went on with the procedure of the ritual. But it was not long before he was in complete samadhi, and so also was the one who was being worshipped. In the stillness of the night both worshipper and worshipped became merged in the Absolute. Hours passed before either came down to the plane of consciousness even in a faint measure. After that Sri Ramakrishna finished the rest of the ritual, dedicating the fruits of all his past and present worship to the Deity. This was the culmination of the sadhana of Sri Ramakrishna. After this he performed no special form of spiritual practice.

The Holy Mother lived at Dakshineswar for another year after this worship. But what an ordeal it was to stay with Sri Ramakrishna! Often he would fall into samadhi and pass the whole night in that state, and she had an anxious time. One night Sri Ramakrishna was so deep in samadhi that one might take him to be dead. In great anxiety the Holy Mother had to send information to others for help. It was a long time before

he could be brought down to the normal plane
by the repeated utterance of sacred mantras. After
regaining external consciousness, when Sri Ramakrishna knew all that had happened, he understood how the Holy Mother was passing night
after night in sleepless anxiety on his account.
Henceforth he arranged that she should stay at
night with his mother at the Nahabat.

    After staying in all for a little more than a year
at Dakshineswar, the Holy Mother returned to
Jayrambati via Kamarpukur in the middle of 1873.
At Jayrambati she again began her usual work—
helping the family in manifold household duties.

    Within a few months, in March 1874, this
happy family at Jayrambati suffered a great loss:
Ram Chandra Mukhopadhyaya, the father of the
Holy Mother, died leaving the already poor family virtually stranded. Shyamasundari, the pious
wife of Ram Chandra, was not a soul to be
daunted by any difficulty. With great faith in the
goodness of God she shouldered the responsibility of the family calmly and bravely. To supplement the slender resources of the family,
Shyamasundari began to husk paddy for a
neighbouring family. During this hour of crisis
the Holy Mother stood by her mother and was a
source of great strength. She did all that was
possible to relieve her mother's great burden. She
would also take care of her younger brothers and

help her unsophisticated mother with advice in many things. Gradually the financial condition of the family improved and the crisis was tided over.

VI
FAITH AND INNOCENCE

In April 1874, the Holy Mother came to
Dakshineswar again. During this second stay she
fell ill of dysentery and suffered terribly. Through
the devoted services of Shambhu Mallick and the
medical care arranged by him she recovered sufficiently to go to her village home in September
1875. There again she had a severe relapse, so
much so that her life was despaired of. She could
hardly walk and her body was reduced to a skel-
eton. She was frightened at seeing her own
reflection in the water—such mere skin and bone
she had become. When the news reached
Dakshineswar, Sri Ramakrishna himself was
anxious and remarked to Hriday, his nephew,
'Coming to earth, will she leave it without having realized the goal of life?'

As all human remedies failed, in great des-
peration one night she went with the help of her
brother Umesh to the village temple of the Divine
Mother, called Simhavahini, where she lay down
vow to fast till the goddess cured her. As she lay
there, she saw the vision of Simhavahini who

appeared before her and suggested a medicine for her eyes which when tried had an immediate effect. The goddess appeared similarly to Shyamasundari Devi and suggested another medicine for dysentery by taking which the Holy Mother completely recovered. As the news of her miraculous cure spread, the Deity began to receive the worship of people from far and near. Even now the temple retains this popularity.

After about a year the Holy Mother again fell ill and suffered this time from an enlargement of the spleen. Following the ways of the village people, Shyamasundari took her daughter to a neighbouring Shiva temple where a quack used to brand the region of the spleen with a piece of burning jujube wood. This drastic remedy was tried. One cannot say whether it had any effect, but what was noteworthy was that the Holy Mother withstood the severe treatment with incredible calm and fortitude, no one even being required to hold her limbs at that time. Gradually she recovered.

The Holy Mother went to Dakshineswar for the third time in January 1877. Perhaps on this (or may be on one of her other visits to Dakshineswar), an incident happened which showed how spiritual innocence is a great power, and guileless confidence placed even in an evil character can transform a life. On the journey from Jayrambati to Dakshineswar one had to cross vast fields. Once the Holy Mother was overtaken by darkness in one of those fields. The whole of her party had gone ahead quickly as night was fast approaching, but she could not keep pace with them. The path had the notoriety of being infested with dacoits and many wayfarers are said to have been robbed of their all and even killed. The Holy Mother was trudging on wearily. At that dark hour she saw a tall figure with a club on his shoulder approaching her. As he came near he sharply asked her where she was going at that hour. In all her innocence the Holy Mother said, 'Father, I am going to Dakshineswar where your son-in-law stays. I have been left behind by my party.' Soon she found approaching a woman who was presumably the man's wife. Her she accosted as mother and told the same thing. The man and woman were so moved by the guileless attitude of Saradamani that they took her to a shop for shelter and fed her with puffed rice bought from the shopkeeper. As no bedding could be had, the woman spread her own clothes and on that laid her 'daughter' to sleep. The couple belonged to a very low caste, but in their great affection for Saradamani they altogether forgot their difference of social position. The next morning they went with her as far as Tarakeshwar, where she met her companions.

By staying only one night with them, she made them so dear to her that they actually began to weep when they had to leave her. Before taking leave, the Holy Mother got a promise from them that they would visit her and their 'son-in-law' at Dakshineswar. This promise was fulfilled, and Sri Ramakrishna treated them as if they were actually his parents-in-law at Dakshineswar. The Holy Mother used to say later that however nice and kind her 'dacoit father' had been to her, she had no doubt that he had committed many acts of robbery.

The Holy Mother had to live alone at Dakshineswar this time since her mother-in-law Chandramani Devi had passed away on February 27, 1876. Meanwhile the great devotee Shambhu Mallick had built a cottage for her on an adjoining piece of land, where she could live a bit more comfortably. There she would stay and cook for the Master. But as Sri Ramakrishna fell ill of dysentery, she again shifted to the Nahabat so that she could take better care of him.

VII
DAKSHINESWAR DAYS

For about thirteen years the Holy Mother lived at Dakshineswar with short intervals now and then when she would go to Jayrambati. At her father's house she lived a very hard life, but her life at Dakshineswar was even harder. Whereas at Jayrambati she had freedom of movement and always enjoyed fresh air, at Dakshineswar she was cooped up in the Nahabat, a small room not more than fifty square feet in area. The Master himself used to say, 'When a free bird is kept imprisoned in a cage its health suffers,' and he was anxious about her health. So considerate was he that when there was nobody near the Nahabat at noon, he would ask the Holy Mother to visit the ladies of the locality and escort her as far as the temple gate. She would return in the evening when the service began in the temple and all people would be drawn there. She was very shy by nature, and hardly anybody could see her though she lived at Dakshineswar for such a long time. An officer of the temple once remarked, 'We have heard she lives there, but never have we seen her.' She would get up very early in the morning, at about three or four, attend to her ablutions, including a bath in the Ganga, and enter her tiny room from where she would come out, if there was any necessity, only at night when people were away. This went on day after day. The door of the room was so low that she had to bend far down to enter. In the beginning she had hard knocks on her head while going in, but afterwards, she said, she got accustomed to the height and avoided injury. This small room was her bedroom, kitchen, storeroom, and everything else. Even on slings she would hang part of her store. Sometimes she had to accommodate other companions here too, mainly the women disciples of Sri Ramakrishna. Ladies from Calcutta who came to visit Sri Ramakrishna would take pity on the Holy Mother and say: 'See, our good girl has to live in such a small room. She is, as it were, in exile like Sita.' In the beginning, she had to cook only for two or three persons, her mother-in-law, the Master, and the like. But as the number of devotees of Sri Ramakrishna began to swell she had to cook for more and more persons. On a birthday of the Master, she had to cook for forty or fifty persons in that room. Sometimes she had to cook to suit different tastes. Naren (afterwards Swami Vivekananda) would like thick gram soup, Ramchandra would ask for chapatis, Rakhal preferred khichuri. Sometimes at odd hours she had to arrange meals for devotees. But the Holy Mother was always equal to the occasion. She was never ruffled, never annoyed. She was sweetness itself and all motherliness.

With how much care did she attend to the needs of the Master! She was all attention to him. In external behaviour Sri Ramakrishna was just like a child. She had to coax and cajole him to take food. He would be frightened if the quantity of rice in his plate looked large. She would therefore press the heap so carefully that it would look small. She would thicken the milk by boiling, so that he could not judge what quantity of milk he was taking. Sometimes she had to suppress the truth about the quantity of food he took; she said that it was not wrong to take the help of a fib as regards food under such circumstances. Sri Ramakrishna used to say jokingly that there was this great need of having a wife: she can cook for the husband. When the Holy Mother was away, he would be in difficulty and feel nervous, for nobody else could take sufficient care of him. The Holy Mother and Sri Ramakrishna stayed in two rooms about seventy-five feet apart; but sometimes they would not meet for months. Still what a great warmth of feeling existed between them! The idea of husband and wife was completely obliterated between the two, but no married love

could compare with the great intensity of love
that they had for each other. A little headache of
the Holy Mother would make the Master anxious
and he would say: 'Ramlal (Sri Ramakrishna's
nephew), what shall we do? She has a headache.'
Some unknown critics raised the question that Sri
Ramakrishna in his quest after the Infinite was
unkind to his wife inasmuch as he did not live a
married life. But no wife on earth has been the
recipient of so much love and consideration from
her husband as Saradamani received from Sri
Ramakrishna.

The relationship between Sri Ramakrishna
and the Holy Mother was not without humour.
Once while she was staying in the cottage built
by Shambhu Mallick, Sri Ramakrishna went to
her in the evening, but as it started raining heavily
he could not again return to his own room that
night. At this Sri Ramakrishna remarked to her, 'I
am staying here just as the temple priests go to
their family houses.' Once a woman came to Sri
Ramakrishna in great agony of mind seeking
peace. Sri Ramakrishna sent her to the Nahabat
saying that in that house lived one who knew the
remedy. When the woman approached the Holy
Mother and repeated what Sri Ramakrishna had
said, she understood the joke that was being
played upon her. The Holy Mother explained to
the woman that she was nothing and that Sri

Ramakrishna was everything and sent her back to him. This was repeated a couple of times. At last the Holy Mother gave the woman a *bilva* leaf used in worship, which had a miraculous effect on her life.

Once there was a controversy as to who between Sri Ramakrishna and another person was fairer in complexion, and Sri Ramakrishna proposed that the Holy Mother should be the umpire. Both the competitors walked side by side in front of the Nahabat so that she might see and judge. Observing strict impartiality, she gave the verdict in favour of the other person, and Sri Ramakrishna lost the contest.

In the early hours of the morning Sri Ramakrishna used to rouse from sleep the Holy Mother and his niece Lakshmi Devi, who then lived with her, so that they might sit for meditation. If there was no response from inside or he suspected that they were asleep, he poured water through the door and quietly walked away.

Above all, her stay in Dakshineswar was a period of great spiritual training. As mentioned before, she would get up every day between three and four in the morning and after a bath in the Ganga begin her meditation. The whole day would be spent in devoted service to the Master, and again in the evening she would practise meditation. In this respect she was mercilessly strict with herself. As she narrated afterwards, one day she was out of sorts and thought it was legitimate to get up late. This she did, and the next day also the same action was repeated. Following this practice for two or three days, she found that she had become an unconscious victim of lethargy. After that she would get up at the fixed time whatever might be her health. This she followed throughout her whole life. Even in times of severe illness, unless quite disabled, she would get up in the early hours and meditate. To the loving remonstrances of her anxious attendants at her being so strict with herself even in old age, she would pay no heed. Once at Dakshineswar while going to the bathing ghat so early in the morning, she almost stumbled upon a crocodile lying on the steps. It got alarmed by her footsteps and jumped into the river. After that when going to the Ganga she would carry a lantern. Seeing the reflection of the moon on the water of the Ganga she would pray, 'There are dark spots even on the moon, but do Thou, O Lord, make me absolutely spotless.' On moonlit nights she would fervently pray that she might be as pure as the light of the moon.

VIII
FORESHADOWING THE FUTURE

It is needless to say that her innate spiritual
longing combined with hard sadhana, and above
all the guidance of a personality like that of Sri
Ramakrishna, had a tremendous effect on the life
of Sarada Devi. But she had a great capacity to
hide her achievements in that sphere. Swami
Premananda, an intimate disciple of the Master,
once remarked that even Sri Ramakrishna had
external manifestations of his spiritual powers in
the form of constant samadhi, but the Holy
Mother had so much control over herself that
nobody knew what a mine of spirituality she pos-
sessed. Carefully suppressing all outward manifestations she lived like an ordinary woman doing
the usual household duties of a poor middle-class
home.

Once the Holy Mother asked Yogin-Ma, a
devotee and her companion, to request the Master to see that she (the Holy Mother) might have
the bliss of samadhi. When Yogin-Ma broached
the subject to Sri Ramakrishna he looked grave
and Yogin-Ma dared not say anything further. But

as she came to the Nahabat she found the Holy Mother seated at her worship, laughing and weeping alternately and tears rolling down her cheeks. Gradually she became quiet and lost in herself. Evidently it was a state of samadhi. Afterwards she asked the Holy Mother, 'How is it, Mother, that you deceived me by saying you had no experience of samadhi?' The Mother simply smiled and did not utter any words. In later days while the Holy Mother, Yogin-Ma and Golap-Ma, another devotee, were meditating on the terrace of a house where they stayed at Belur, the Holy Mother was found to have lost all outward consciousness, so deep was her meditation. After some time, regaining partial consciousness, she said, 'O Yogin, where are my limbs?' Yogin-Ma narrated afterwards that they began to press her hands and feet to convince her they existed. It was long before she came down to the normal plane.

Only those who were very intimate with her could witness one or two incidents which revealed her real spiritual stature, but to all others she was only a mother.

Her motherliness, which afterwards like a huge banyan tree gave shelter and refuge to enumerable weary souls, showed signs of manifesting even in her early days at Dakshineswar. So much so, that sometimes the mother in her got the better of her devotion even to the Master. There were occasions when impelled by motherly feelings she would overrule even the wishes and desires of Sri Ramakrishna.

Once a woman came to Dakshineswar. She was supposed to be just a crank but afterwards was found to be practising sadhana according to madhura bhava, that is, in the attitude of looking upon God as a husband. She one day said that she cherished the same attitude towards Sri Ramakrishna. The Master got wild at hearing such words and began to rebuke her so loudly that it created a sensation. At this the Holy Mother sent for the woman, treated her lovingly as if she were her own daughter, and said: 'If he gets annoyed at your presence, you need not go to him. Just come to me.'

Another woman was in the habit of coming to the Nahabat to have the pleasure and benefit of the company of the Holy Mother. This woman had lived an impure life in her younger days, and for this reason the Master told the Holy Mother not to associate with her. But the woman would come to the Holy Mother just as to a mother for solace and consolation. How could a mother reject her daughter, however bad? The Holy Mother paid no heed to the protests of the Master, and the lady continued to come to the Nahabat. The Master noticed this, but raised no further objection, presumably understanding the feelings and attitude of the Holy Mother.

Sri Ramakrishna was very strict with his young disciples as regards diet, spiritual practices, etc. One day he learnt that Baburam (afterwards Swami Premananda) took five or six chapatis at night. That was too many, he thought, and asked why he took such a large quantity at night. The young boy replied that the Holy Mother served them to him. Then Sri Ramakrishna went to the Holy Mother and took her to task for thus spoiling the spiritual prospects of the boys. At this the Holy Mother replied: 'You need not worry about their welfare. I will look to that.' The Master saw the sentiment behind these words and simply laughed. Could a mother refuse to give sufficient quantity of food to her children? That was impossible.

Sri Ramakrishna was aware of the spiritual powers that were hers. Though now and then he would give her spiritual instructions just as to a disciple, at other times he would consider her as his peer, or one on whom his spiritual mantle would fall. 'People are living like worms in darkness; you will have to look after them,' he once said to her. On another occasion he said to her in an appealing tone, 'Am I to do everything alone, and will you not do anything?' 'What can I do?' asked the Holy Mother. 'You can do a lot,' replied

Sri Ramakrishna.

One day the Master actually sent a young boy—Sarada, afterwards Swami Trigunatitananda—to the Holy Mother for spiritual initiation, quoting a Vaishnava couplet which says that Radha is infinitely more powerful than Sri Krishna.

The chief trait in the character of Sri Ramakrishna, according to the Holy Mother, was renunciation. People generally say that his greatest achievement was the harmonization of all faiths. But this paled into insignificance, in the opinion of his life-companion, when compared with his spirit of renunciation. But her own renunciation was just as great. One day a rich Marwari devotee proposed to put a big amount in the bank to the credit of Sri Ramakrishna so that he might not have any financial worry about his needs. Sri Ramakrishna was perturbed at the very proposal as if it was an abysmal fall from the ideal to which he was pledged. When hard pressed by the devotee to accept the money, the Master, just to test the Holy Mother's mind, had her brought there and proposed that the money might be kept in her name if she agreed. She also adamantly refused the offer as that would be tantamount to the acceptance of the money by the Master himself. Sri Ramakrishna was so glad to see her sensitiveness to the ideal!

In later days when the Holy Mother went on a pilgrimage to South India, the Raja of Ramnad, a disciple of Swami Vivekananda, ordered the temple staff to show her his jewelry and request her to accept anything she liked as that would be conferring a great favour upon him. The Holy Mother shuddered at the very idea, but at repeated requests said that Radhu, her niece who accompanied her on the pilgrimage, might take something she liked. But even then she was praying silently to the Lord that Radhu might not cause embarrassment to her by showing covetousness. Radhu, to the Holy Mother's great relief, asked only for a lead-pencil to replace one that she had lost.

...

IX
THE PASSING OF
SRI RAMAKRISHNA

A precept which the Holy Mother used to
emphasize greatly was that one should learn how
to adjust oneself to time and circumstances—for
therein lies the secret of peace and happiness in
life. She herself was the living embodiment of this
saying. Born and brought up in a village atmosphere, she was quite at home at Dakshineswar.
But harder days were ahead of her.

In June 1885, Sri Ramakrishna developed can-
cer of the throat, and this necessitated his removal
in October to Shyampukur in Calcutta for treatment. The devotees arranged for everything
regarding medical care, nursing, and so on. They
knew that an expert hand would be needed to
take charge of his diet. The Holy Mother was at
Dakshineswar. She would be the best one to be
entrusted with that responsibility. But how would
she be able to stay in the small crowded house
where Sri Ramakrishna was accommodated and
where there was no other woman? This was their
misgiving. When the proposal reached her

however, she at once came to Shyampukur to do
the best she could for the Master. A small shed on
the terrace of the second storey was allotted to
her, where she would stay during the day and
far into the night. When all were asleep at night,
she would come down a to a room on the first
floor and sleep for three hours at most there and
then return to her place on the terrace. When it
was necessary to feed or otherwise attend on Sri
Ramakrishna, she would come to him. Thus she
lived from day to day, without the slightest
thought of any personal suffering, her only prayer
being that the Master might regain his health, no
matter what might be her inconvenience.

As there was no sign of improvement in his
illness, Sri Ramakrishna was shifted to Cossipore
in December 1885. The Holy Mother also accompanied him there, and occupied herself day and
night in attending to his needs. The young disciples also sacrificed all other thoughts and were
doing their utmost to save the life of their beloved
Master. The prolonged illness of Sri Ramakrishna
had a great deal to do with the building up of the
future Ramakrishna brotherhood; for, while serving the Master in that hour of distress, the young
disciples felt the bond of love growing among
them all the more strongly. If that is true, it en-
sured also the place of Sarada Devi in the future
Order. The young disciples, the future builders

of the Ramakrishna Order, though they had little opportunity of talking with her, began to look upon Sarada Devi as their own mother; and their reverence for her was equalled only by that for the Master.

Sri Ramakrishna was sinking. The Holy Mother got some premonition that the end was near. Still she was hoping against hope that the disease might be arrested and the Master might recover. But death is no respecter of persons and is not swayed by any human sentiment or feelings. Sri Ramakrishna passed into Mahasamadhi on 16 August 1886, plunging all his disciples and devotees into profound grief and gloom.

On the following day, when the Holy Mother was preparing to wear the widow's garments, Sri Ramakrishna appeared before her and said: 'What are you doing? Where have I gone? It is like passing from one room to another.' At this the Holy Mother was a bit consoled and gave up the idea of putting on the widow's dress. But as a sign of her grief she tore off a large portion of the wide red border of her sari. Afterwards she attempted once or twice to remove the gold ornaments she had on her hands, but every time she was prevented by the appearance of Sri Ramakrishna before her. The last time she attempted this was at Kamarpukur. There to save herself from the village gossip, she took off her bracelets. But one day there too she saw the vision of the Master. At this experience she shook off all fear of public criticism, and henceforth she wore simple bracelets on her hands and used a narrow-bordered cloth for her wearing apparel.

After the demise of the Master, some devotees proposed that the establishment at Cossipore should be broken up immediately. But Naren and the other young disciples objected as that would be an additional shock to the Mother. So the establishment remained there for some days more, till August 21, when the Holy Mother went to stay at the house of Balaram Bose, the great devotee of the Master. There was some trouble and misunderstanding between the sannyasin and householder disciples as regards the possession of the relics of the Master. When the news reached the Holy Mother she remarked: 'Such a unique person is gone. But they are quarrelling over his ashes!'

X

TRIALS AND SUFFERINGS

Shortly after, on 30 August 1886, accompanied by a party of devotees, the Mother started on a pilgrimage to North India to assuage her grief. On the way she stopped at Deoghar, Varanasi, and Ayodhya, and went as far as Vrindavan, where she stayed for about a year. While she was witnessing the evening service at the temple of Vishwanath at Varanasi, she fell into an ecstatic mood and that mood persisted even while she was returning to her place of lodging. At Varanasi she met the great saint, Swami Bhaskarananda, and was much impressed by him.

At Vrindavan she practised hard tapasya, and her feelings were greatly stirred by the sight of the places associated with Sri Krishna, Radha and his other companions. Was not her case exactly like that of Radha when she was separated from her Lord? When she met Yogin-Ma at Vrindavan, where she had gone earlier, she began to weep like a helpless child. That mood lasted for a few days till she was pacified by having a vision of the Master. At Vrindavan she would be so much absorbed in japa and meditation that she was not conscious at the time that flies were making sores on her face. Sometimes in an exalted mood she would go alone to the sandy banks of the Yamuna, from where her companions had to bring her back. It is said that at Kala Babu's house she was so absorbed in samadhi that she could be brought down to the earthly plane only with considerable effort, by repeatedly uttering the name of the Lord in her ears. These high spiritual moods would alternate with simple and unsophisticated behaviour just like that of an innocent child. She visited almost all the important temples in that holy city, some of them several times. She once circumambulated the sacred area associated with Sri Krishna's life on foot, just like the orthodox Vaishnavas, although she was suffering from rheumatism. Her companions noticed that at many places sanctified by the memory of Sri Krishna she would experience an exalted mood.

While staying at Vrindavan, she once saw a vision in which the Master was asking her to give initiation to Swami Yogananda who was then staying with her as her attendant. At first she paid no attention to the vision, but the experience recurred on three consecutive days. Out of humility she hesitated to give initiation to anyone, but when she learnt that the Master had not given Yogananda any formal initiation and that he too had a vision similar to hers, she agreed and initiated him. Perhaps this was the first initiation she gave to anybody, for it is not definitely known whether she initiated Sarada (Swami Trigunatitananda) whom the Master sent to her for that purpose at Dakshineswar.

At the temple of Radharani in Vrindavan she fervently prayed that her eyes might not see faults in others. That her prayer was answered was borne out in her life. Just as a mother cannot see any fault in her child, she was incapable of seeing any blemish in anyone. Afterwards she would advise everyone to try not to see defects in others for, as she would say, one's own eyes become impure and one absorbs the defects of others.

After one year's stay at Vrindavan she went to Hardwar, and returned to Calcutta after visiting Jaipur, Ajmere, and Allahabad on the way.

After a temporary halt in Calcutta for two days, she started for Kamarpukur accompanied by Swami Yogananda and Golap-Ma, both of whom came back to Calcutta after a few days.

Now began a period of great trial and hardship for her. At this time she had no financial resources and almost nobody to take care of her. She felt a void in her heart at the physical absence of the Master, and she was lonely. She was faced with so much poverty that at times she had to eat rice without even salt. The disciples of the Master had been seized with spiritual longing and impelled by that spirit wandered from place to place; so they did not know the sufferings of the Holy Mother, nor did it strike any of them that there was a possibility that she might be in such great difficulty. The Holy Mother also would not speak of her personal hardships to anybody. Faith in God was her only refuge and support. Once at repeated invitations of her mother she went to Jayrambati. Shyamasundari Devi at once found out the abject poverty through which she was passing, but could not extract from her the actual condition. She tried her best to keep her daughter at Jayrambati, but the Holy Mother would not agree to stay. She returned to her husband's birthplace just to wait and see how circumstances would shape themselves for her.

Despite all her attempts to hide the real situation the news leaked out to the outside world that she was passing through a period of great privation. When the devotees in Calcutta heard about it they became alarmed and grave. After consulting among themselves they wrote to the Holy Mother earnestly requesting her to come to Calcutta. But there was this difficulty. Whatever might be her spiritual relation with the disciples of the Master, what would the villagers think if she went to Calcutta to stay among strangers, as they would say? At last, at the persuasion of an elderly woman in Kamarpukur who commanded great reverence from all, and also with the support of her mother, she went to Calcutta. Great relief and joy was felt by the devotees, especially the women disciples.

Henceforth she lived sometimes in Calcutta and sometimes at Jayrambati according to convenience and circumstances, except in the periods when she was on pilgrimage.

XI
PILGRIMAGES

In November 1888, Holy Mother went to Puri in a party including Yogin-Ma and Swamis Brahmananda, Yogananda and Saradananda. As a mark of honour and respect to her, Govinda Shringeri, the priest of Balaram Bose's family at Puri, wanted to take her to the Jagannath temple in a palanquin. But the proposal did not appeal to her at all. She preferred to go on foot as a humble devotee to see Jagannath, the Lord of the Universe. She stayed for more than two months in Puri visiting the temple often in the mornings and evenings and spending much time in meditation in the shrine of Lakshmi. As Sri Ramakrishna had not visited Puri during his lifetime, she once took a photograph of the Master to the temple and showed the image of Jagannath to it. The Master was such a living reality to her.

In March 1890, she went to Gaya with Swami Advaitananda, a disciple of the Master. She visited Bodh Gaya, the place where Buddha had enlightenment. At Bodh Gaya there was a Hindu monastery. Seeing the perfect living arrangements in the institution, she prayed to the Master that her children, i.e. the monastic disciples of Sri Ramakrishna, instead of wandering about from place to place as they were then doing, might find a permanent place of shelter and that they might not have to struggle so hard to meet their bare physical requirements. She used to say that through the grace of the Master the monastery at Belur was established soon afterward. In 1895 she visited Varanasi and Vrindavan for the second time, accompanied by her mother and brothers. And in 1904 she revisited Puri—this time with Swami Premananda, some devotees of the Master and some of her relations.

In the year 1910 she went on a pilgrimage to South India. On the way she stopped for two months at Kothar, in Orissa, at the home of Balaram Bose. At Kothar, Devendra Nath Chatterjee, the local postmaster, who had accepted Christianity, came repentant to the Holy Mother. The Holy Mother always knew how to rise equal to the occasion. She advised him to get reconverted to Hinduism, which he did. Afterwards she directed one of her monastic followers to give him the sacred thread and the Gayatri Mantra, and she herself gave him spiritual initiation.

The following February in a party of eight she started for Madras. Swami Ramakrishnananda, the head of the Ramakrishna Math at Madras, made all arrangements for her continuing pilgrimage in the South. She stayed for a month in the city of Madras. Innumerable women devotees would flock to her every day, and though she could not talk to them in their own language, they felt the touch of her affection and the favour of her blessings nonetheless. From Madras she started for Madura, Swami Ramakrishnananda himself conducting the party. After visiting the Minakshi temple and other notable places, they visited Rameshwaram where they stayed for three days. By special order of the Raja of Ramnad she was given facilities for worship which no other pilgrim was privileged to have. The Raja of Ramnad did all in his power to show her the highest respect and honour.

From Rameshwaram the party went to Bangalore, where a branch of the Ramakrishna Math had already been established. Holy Mother's presence at Bangalore created a great stir, and even without any public announcement a large number of people would visit the Ashrama every day to have her *darshan* and blessings. The visitors showered so many flowers at her feet that they often lay in heaps. All these tributes she took as due to the influence of the Master, which had by that time spread far and wide and it made her very happy.

She returned to Calcutta in April 1911, halt-

She returned to Calcutta in April 1911, halting for a day at Rajahmundry to have a bath in the Godavari and for two days at Puri again to have the darshan of Jagannath.

The last pilgrimage she undertook was in 1912, when she visited Varanasi for the third time in a large party consisting of some senior monks, devotees, and a few of her relations. On this occasion she stayed at Varanasi for about two and a half months and so could visit at leisure all the important temples and sacred places around the city. During her stay at Varanasi she met the well-known saint Chameli Puri. She was so much impressed by the spiritual power and withal the childlike appearance of this holy man that she remarked she felt no inclination to go to see any other saint. As a mark of reverence she sent him some fruits, sweets and a blanket.

One day she went to Sarnath, the place where Buddha preached his first sermon, and which is, as such, a sacred place of pilgrimage to the Buddhists. Here she saw many Westerners admiring with interest the ruins of the ancient city. She remarked that the very people who once built those buildings were now admiring them in great wonder.

The Ramakrishna Mission Home of Service at Varanasi had by that time developed into a well-established institution serving the sick and

distressed. She visited it at the earnest prayers of
the workers. As she went round the wards, she
showed great appreciation and said, 'The living
presence of the Master can be felt here.'

The Mother returned to Calcutta in January
1913.

XII
IN CALCUTTA AND AT JAYRAMBATI

Holy Mother during the early period of her
life in Calcutta would stay in rented houses at
various places. For short visits she would put up
at the houses of devotees like Balaram Bose or
M., the celebrated author of *The Gospel of Sri
Ramakrishna*. Sometimes she lived on the western side of the Ganga—once at Ghusuri, and
twice at Nilambar Mukherjee's garden house.[1]
She used to say that from her younger days she
had a great love for the Ganga. While staying at
Nilambar Mukherjee's garden, along with her
companion Yogin-Ma, she performed the
Panchatapa austerity, which consists in sitting for
japa and meditation amidst five fires—four blaz-
ing on four sides and the summer sun above—
from morning to evening for seven consecutive
days. The Mother passed through this fiery ordeal successfully. In this house again once she had

---

[1] Where the Ramakrishna Math was located prior
to shifting to the new Math grounds at Belur Math.

a strange vision. She saw that Sri Ramakrishna was walking into the Ganga. As he was doing so his body melted into the water and Swami Vivekananda began to sprinkle that holy water on innumerable people. This vision made such a vivid impression on her mind that for many days she could not bathe in the river considering its holiness.

It was in 1909 that Swami Saradananda built a permanent home for her in Calcutta at the present No. 1, Udbodhan Lane. Now when in Calcutta the Holy Mother would stay here. This house, bearing the sacred memory and association of the Holy Mother, is known as 'The Mother's House' to innumerable devotees and disciples of the Ramakrishna Order. To how many aspiring souls did she give initiation here! Many are the persons who came weary and heavy-laden to have their lacerated hearts soothed, and got infinite solace. When the Mother would be here, all who stayed in the house and all who visited could get access, as it were, into a world which cannot be reached even by hard tapasya. Now she is physically absent, but the association of her memory with the spot is a source of divine inspiration to thousands of devotees who did not have the privilege of seeing her in her lifetime.

While in Calcutta, the Holy Mother was the centre of spiritual attraction to all, but when she would go to her parental home at Jayrambati, she would adjust herself so well to the home-atmosphere that her relations could hardly realize what a great spiritual personality she was. She was there the familiar sister to her brothers taking anxious care of them, and the same 'Sarada' to the elderly village women who had known her from her childhood. Her adjustment was natural and spontaneous. It was with reference to this characteristic that Sri Ramakrishna once humorously remarked that she was like a cat that hid its colour in ashes. At Jayrambati she would be seen working very hard just like any other woman in a poor village family. So long as her mother was alive, she assisted her in everything. When she died the Holy Mother, being the eldest sister, virtually became the guardian of the family. This meant not only responsibility but also considerable annoyance. The youngest of her brothers, who had some education, died prematurely. The three other brothers were entirely different from their sister. When one saw them, one wondered if they could really be relatives of the Holy Mother. Without education or culture, narrow-minded and selfish, they judged everything in terms of money. Quarrelling among themselves even over petty things, they made the life of the Holy Mother unbearable and taxed her patience to the utmost. But she bore everything with superhuman calmness. Apart from her spiritual attainments, for the way in which she maintained her inner peace amidst the volcanic fury that raged round her at Jayrambati, she should to be considered one of the greatest saints. One day two of her brothers quarrelled most ignominiously over some petty property. The Holy Mother came to pacify them, but when she returned to her room she began to laugh as if she had witnessed great fun and remarked, 'They fight for such small things and do not consider that at death everything will be left behind.'

She had not only to take care of her brothers, but also of her brothers' children whom she had to bring up with her own hand. Nalini, Maku and Radhu, three of her nieces, were her constant companions. And there was Surabala, the widow of her youngest brother, who for her craziness was known as the mad aunt, and who was ever a source of trouble to the Holy Mother. Her brothers found in her a sister whose affection could be exploited in terms of material advantage, and her nieces found in her an aunt who would tolerate any amount of their pranks and eccentricities and fulfil any of their demands. None of them realized that much higher things could be had from her. Once she remarked: 'They always ask for money. Even through mistake they do not ask for knowledge and devotion.'

After the passing away of the Master, when the Holy Mother had been brooding over her lot and feeling that she had no further interest in life, she had a vision of Sri Ramakrishna. She saw a little girl with a red cloth walking in front of her, and the Master, pointing to the child, said, 'Cling to her as a support.' Some years after, once while she was seated at Jayrambati, she saw the insane widow of her youngest brother walking with her neglected infant daughter, Radhu, crawling behind. As the Holy Mother witnessed the pathetic sight, she felt a peculiar sensation in her heart. She at once rushed to the spot and took Radhu in her arms. As she did this she saw the vision of the Master, who appeared before her and said: 'Cling to this child as your mental support on earth. She is Maya.' From this time on, the Holy Mother showed the utmost interest in this girl, and Radhu found in the Mother the embodiment of all earthly love. But as the girl grew up, she proved herself hardly worthy of Holy Mother's love. She was a queer amalgam of obstinacy and innocence, craziness and simplicity. Being of poor health and debilitated mind, she was the constant source of anxiety to the Mother. Radhu's behaviour and mode of life would often be the cause, not only of trouble, but also of great embarrassment; but the Holy Mother's affection for her was, as it were, a tie that did not allow her mind to soar altogether beyond the earthly plane. Towards the end, when the Holy Mother lost all interest in Radhu, her attendants feared that she would not live long. Actually she passed away soon after.

Girish Chandra Ghosh, the great actor-dramatist and a staunch devotee of Sri Ramakrishna, once remarked as he saw the brothers and relations of the Holy Mother, 'These people must have practised great tapasya in their past lives to deserve so much love and affection from the Holy Mother.' This is true. Where hundreds of persons would consider it a life's privilege to be of the slightest service to the Holy Mother, her relatives actually received personal service from the Mother herself.

Sri Ramakrishna, though a prince of monks, never forgot the slightest duty to his wife. And she, too, in her turn, though adored and literally worshipped as the manifestation of Divine Power on earth, welcomed the drudgery, worries and troubles involved in fulfilling her duties to her relatives, however unworthy they might have been of her love. Once she actually said to her brothers, 'You got me as your sister only because of the piety of my father and mother.'

XIII
AS A SPIRITUAL FORCE

There were some devotees who at first would not give much importance to the Holy Mother. 'Sri Ramakrishna might have been a great saint, but his wife did not necessarily share his greatness' was their critical attitude. But gradually as the spiritual personality of the Holy Mother began to unfold, these people had to change their opinions, and their indifference was transformed into great reverence.

Sri Ramakrishna used to say that the sergeant's lamp keeps the sergeant himself in darkness but throws light outside. So to her relations, though the Holy Mother was not worth much more than the worldly advantages she could offer, her spiritual influence spread far and wide. People from all quarters would come to her for solace, guidance, spiritual instruction and initiation. Sri Ramakrishna knew that she would have to do this work in continuation of what he had started, so he gave her special training in that direction. He taught her some mantras—seeds of spiritual growth—made living by his sadhana which she might give to her future disciples. These she gave unreservedly. While Sri Ramakrishna himself would be very particular in choosing a disciple, the Holy Mother, prompted by her motherly heart, could hardly refuse anyone the favour. Swami Premananda, an intimate disciple of Sri Ramakrishna, once remarked: 'The poison which we cannot assimilate, we send to the Holy Mother.' He meant that the people whom they could not control or reform were sent by them to the Holy Mother. And invariably they would turn over a new leaf after receiving her blessings.

For a real guru, to give initiation means receiving the sins of the disciple on himself. The Holy Mother was conscious of this. She had to pay dearly for making innumerable disciples by accepting physical suffering and ailments. But she could not resist the desire to help others. An attendant once argued with the Holy Mother about the desirability of her not giving initiation, as that brought disease on her. At this she remarked, 'Did the Master come only to eat rasagolla (a kind of Bengal sweet)?' Thereby she meant that she also was not born simply to enjoy the sweet things of life.

It was not for nothing that people flocked to her. Innumerable are the persons who got infinite strength from a single utterance from her lips.

Many are the lives which by her influence she saved from a moral crash or a spiritual downfall. She knew how to be equal to the occasion. Outwardly her mode of life was almost similar to that of other women in the village; there was not much to distinguish her. But at times she would rise to her spiritual height, to the wonder and amazement of the people concerned. 'One who has got blessings from me need not worry about final liberation,' 'I and the Master are one.' 'If you meditate on me and remember me, that will be enough.'—Utterances like these would come from her lips when a disciple was found wavering or in distress. Such utterances seemed all the more wonderful when one remembers that she was humility itself and that there was not the least trace of egotism in her. In talks and conversations with her one would always get the impression that she felt she was nothing—the Master was everything. Her unassuming behaviour was so very natural and spontaneous that at times those who were with her felt as if she was no more than a child, even in her advanced age when thousands of people looked to her for guidance, not only in the perplexing situations of this life, but also to solve the problems of the eternal life.

A jewel has different values for different persons. What place the Holy Mother occupied in the spiritual sphere was difficult for ordinary persons to judge. A faint glimpse of that could be had when one saw the attitude to her of some who were undoubtedly known as spiritual geniuses. Vivekananda was emboldened to cross the ocean and go to the West to preach only when he got the blessings of the Holy Mother. Her blessings were enough, he thought, to jump into the uncertainty of whatever might await him in strange lands and still stranger conditions. Swami Brahmananda, one of the most towering personalities of the Ramakrishna Order and the first President of the Ramakrishna Mission, when approaching the Holy Mother, would shake with emotion and behave just like a simple and innocent child. Swami Saradananda, who was the guiding figure behind the Ramakrishna Math and Mission, sincerely felt that the Holy Mother might substitute any other man in his place and that man would be able to do exactly the work he was doing—if not more efficiently. Her blessings were the source of all strength to him. This devotion of the great disciples of Sri Ramakrishna was not merely a form of reverence shown to the wife of their Guru; they literally looked upon her as the manifestation of the Divine Mother incarnate and at times actually worshipped her as such. Swami Brahmananda, who had a great reputation for controlling his spiritual sentiment, once on the occasion of the Durga Puja festival worshipped her with flowers and sacred leaves as one does the Divine Mother. Swami Saradananda would offer similar worship to her on special days reserved for the worship of the Divine Mother. The remarkable thing was that the Holy Mother was the same unassuming person when she received worship from such persons as when she would undergo the drudgery of duties at her parental home at Jayrambati. A woman devotee once remarked: 'How wonderful are the powers of the Holy Mother! When thousands of persons are literally worshipping her, she is completely unattached to the honours that are being showered on her. This is not possible for any human being. It is enough proof of her divinity.'

Though she had little book-learning, her power to solve the intricate problems of spiritual life was remarkable. Her solutions would always go straight to the heart of the questioner and give him sustenance throughout his whole life.

Why there is so much suffering in God's world is a problem which agitates the mind of every devotee. When the Holy Mother was approached with that question, her answer was: 'Creation means a mixture of happiness and misery. Misery is the symbol of God's compassion. Besides, none suffers for all time. Every action brings its inevitable result, and as such the turn for happiness will surely come.'

'Was there any use in repeating God's name if one did not have love for Him?' asked a disciple. 'If you fall into water, whether willingly or unwillingly, your cloth will get wet all the same, will it not?' was her answer that immediately quietened him.

Why does one not experience God-absorption, though one is constantly repeating God's name—is a problem that perplexes a spiritual aspirant occasionally. When the Holy Mother was asked that question, her practical advice was: 'It will come, by and by. But do not give up japa even if the mind is unwilling and unsteady. You must go on with the repetition of the name and you will find that the mind is gradually getting steadier, like a flame in calm air. Any movement in the air disturbs the steady burning of a flame; even so the presence of any thought or desire makes the mind unsteady. The mantra must be correctly repeated. As incorrect utterance delays progress.'

'But, then, a single utterance of the Lord's name is as effective as a million repetitions if you do it with a steady, concentrated mind. What is the use of repeating the mantra a million times with an absent mind? You must do it whole-heartedly. Then only can you deserve his grace,' was her answer to a similar question on another occasion.

'God's grace is shed on all just as the sun's

light is for all. Then what is the use of spiritual practice?'—asked a devotee trying by logical argument to prove the uselessness of sadhana. 'Food-stuffs are there. The one who will cook them earlier will eat earlier; one who does not at all like to cook will go hungry,' was her simple answer forthcoming.

'We see innumerable creations of God. Were they created one by one or otherwise?' was the question that arose in the mind of a young disciple, and he put it to the Mother in childlike innocence. 'God is not like a painter who draws the eyes, face, nose of every figure. No, He does not work that way. He has a unique power. By his mere will the universe comes into being and at his wish it goes to naught. All the things of the universe have been created all at once and not one by one,' was her answer to that difficult philosophical problem.

Among the disciples of Sri Ramakrishna, Girish Chandra Ghosh had argumentative powers and a combative nature only second to those of Swami Vivekananda. Seized by an impulsive desire to embrace sannyasa, he once went to the Holy Mother at Jayrambati to ask for her permission. With all his natural vehemence he began to argue with the Mother to obtain her approval for his resolve. But she withstood all his arguments and with her quiet answers completely broke his resolution. Her insight into the spiritual nature of persons was very unerring. An important member of the Ramakrishna Order went to her for initiation when young. For a long he had been worshipping a particular deity as his Chosen Ideal but the Mother gave him a different Ideal. When he said that he had for a long time been worshipping another Ideal, she replied quietly: 'No, that is not the Ideal for you. Follow what I have given.' And in a short time the disciple found her words to be true. The same disciple, some time later, suffered from brain-fag as he had strained too much in spiritual practices. As a remedy he tried various things, consulted many physicians, but to r ɔ effect. The senior monks of the Order were concerned about his problem but could not give any effective help. He soon went to Jayrambati to the Holy Mother. When he narrated the details of his case, she shuddered to hear of the method which he followed in his meditation. Ah, it was dangerous for him! She corrected his method of meditation, and he was all right in no time.

It was not for nothing that Holy Mother's word was the final word in everything spiritual and secular concerning the Ramakrishna Math and Mission. Her advice, her decision, a mere wish of hers, was like a sacred injunction from on high to the monks and devotees of the Order. This attitude of theirs only deepened as time passed.

XIV
THE ALL-LOVING MOTHER

In her life was found a wonderful mixture of the human and the divine. Apart from her spiritual power, the mere human aspects of her life were enough to make her an exemplary character in the eyes of the world. She was indeed the final word in the perfection of Indian womanhood. Her actions always showed the highest dignity and greatest magnanimity. Not even through mistake could she associate herself with anything small or narrow. Even in her ordinary dealings she was head and shoulders above all others in refinement and broadness of outlook. Her life was always a model for others to follow, and it was difficult to find the least trace of imperfection in her actions and behaviour.

But the most dominant trait in her character, overshadowing every other feature, was her motherly love. She might be anything else, but everybody found in her a mother—only her love was stronger than that of one's own mother. Many young men who had lost their mothers early in life, and did not know what a mother's love was, had their loss more than compensated when they came in touch with her. Many, after finding a mother in her, did not hanker after anything else in this life or in the life to come. Her love was enough to give them security here and salvation hereafter. They did not even care to know of her spiritual powers. They did not care to see the highest of the Himalayan peaks when they felt themselves sufficiently blessed by touching the foot of that great mountain. There was something in her attitude which soon disarmed all fear and awe. While she was giving initiation, perhaps the disciple was struck with awe and overwhelmed with a feeling of reverence; but once the initiation was over, when she would feed him with sweets just like his own mother, he would at once be just as free with her as he was at his own home. There were instances when she gave her own clothes or blankets to young disciples for their use. Perhaps these disciples would think it sacrilegious to use things which the Mother had used. But her spontaneous motherly attitude would at once remove any such feelings. Does a son hesitate to use anything which his mother gives him? At Jayrambati she would cook for the devotees, wash their plates and cleanse the place they ate. Devotees would sometimes come from a distance, and after staying only two or three days with her would feel so much drawn

to her that they would shed tears while leaving
the place. Sometimes as they departed the Mother
would watch them, as far as they could be seen,
with eyes moistened with the tears of a mother's
love. Once a young monk who stayed with her
went out on some business. It was almost evening
when he returned. But the Mother would not take
her meal before he came. How could a mother
take her food when the son had not had his![1]
When the disciple saw this, he was overwhelmed
with emotion. Even one's own mother is not
always so considerate! She was the mother of all.
Every soul born of the womb of a woman would
find in her a mother. Her love knew no distinc-
tion of caste, creed or geographical boundaries.
People from the East and West, from the South
and the North would come to her to receive her
blessings. She might not even be able to speak
their language. But the unspoken language of her
love was more than enough for them—they
would feel blessed.

When Sister Nivedita came to India, Swami
Vivekananda was a bit anxious about how to
make a place for her in Hindu society. But the
Holy Mother accommodated her in her own
room. It took tremendous courage and extreme

---

[1] Typical behaviour of a traditional Hindu mother.

broad-mindedness on the part of the Mother, for if the news reached her relations she might have to face social persecution. Was it not remarkable, even for herself, that although she belonged to an orthodox Brahmin family and lacked modern education, she could allow an European lady to stay with her? And that too, in the last century at a time when Hindu society was uncompromising in its rigidity as regards social rules!

Though she belonged to an old world, as it were, hers was an extremely modern mind. Seeing this trait in her, Sister Nivedita very aptly remarked, 'Is she the last of an old order or the beginning of a new?' Many a non-Bengali or non-Indian devotee would go to the Holy Mother, but so great was the breadth of her innate culture that everyone would feel quite at home with her. Once while listening to Easter music at Sister Nivedita's place she became so absorbed that one wondered how, without knowing any western language, she could enter so much into the spirit of the resurrection hymns. Similarly, when the English marriage ritual was being described to her once, her face lit up with joy as she heard the marriage vow, 'For better, for worse, for richer, for poorer, in sickness and in health—till death us do part,' and she exclaimed, 'Oh, the *dharmi* words! the righteous words!'

Her mental penetration was so very keen and

her common sense so strong that even in things supposedly outside her sphere she could give a very sound opinion. During the first World War, a disciple told the Mother how President Wilson was trying to ensure the peace of the whole world and prevent war in the future. The Mother's quiet remark was, 'They all speak through the lips and not from the heart.' Once a disciple was telling her of the many facilities of life which the British rule had given to India. Her reply, however, was, 'But is it not a fact that the poverty of the people is increasing more and more?'

Sometimes people belonging to inferior castes would come to her at Jayrambati, but her same-sighted attitude towards them would always be unchanged. Only, she would see that they observed the usual caste restrictions in the presence of others, as otherwise there could be a sensation in the village where orthodoxy prevailed.

A coolie-woman came to her one evening with some vegetables sent by a devotee, and had to stop for the night at the house. The woman had fever at night and vomited. Next morning before others awakened the Holy Mother washed the soiled bedding so that the poor woman might not be scolded by anyone.

A Mohammedan, engaged as a labourer, was one day taking a meal in her house. He sat on the

verandah of the house. Nalini, a niece of the
Mother, was serving him. Owing to caste preju-
dices Nalini remained at a distance and began to
throw the food on the plate of the man. At this
the Holy Mother reprimanded her niece and herself served him the meal. After he had finished,
the Mother cleansed the spot where he had taken
his food. Nalini was shocked and exclaimed:
'What are you doing? Will you not lose caste by
this?'

In Calcutta, Radhu fell ill, and two famous
physicians treated her. The Holy Mother directed
Radhu to take the dust of the feet of the physicians as a mark of respect, though they belonged
to a lower caste.

Instances are not uncommon when people of
extremely low caste received initiation from her
and afterwards sat for their meals in her own
room and Mother herself washed their plates.
According to social custom it would be considered sinful for them to receive such services from
a brahmin. Under ordinary circumstances they
themselves would not have stood that. But they
felt that she was their very mother, and so what
harm if she rendered them such services! It was
but natural.

She felt very intensely the poverty and suffering of people in general. She would take great
interest in the social service activities of the Rama-

krishna Mission. If a monk came to her with a complaint that such work interfered with his meditative life, she would pay no attention to him. 'These are also the Master's works,' she would say. While at Jayrambati she would take a sympathetic interest in the affairs of all the neighbours and was a source of great strength to them. Her compassion and timely help would lighten their burden of sufferings.

Though kindness itself, she was not slow to show indignation when occasion demanded it. When two young women, one of whom was an expectant mother, were made on political suspicion to walk a long distance by the local police and the news reached the Holy Mother, she got extremely upset. 'Is this due to Government orders or the over-zeal of the police officials? Were there no men near by to rescue the poor girls?' she said, greatly agitated in mind. Afterwards she was glad to hear that the women were released.

Even persons who had gone astray did not fail to receive her love and blessings, sometimes even inspite of the meek protests of other devotees. Once she bluntly said, 'If my son rolls in the dust, even then he is my child.' On another occasion she said, 'I am as much the mother of the good as of the bad.' Once a woman who felt guilty of moral turpitude came to see her in Calcutta but dared not enter her room. The Mother understood the whole thing. She herself brought her into her room, caressed her and gave her initiation. 'What if you have done anything wrong? When you are repentant your guilt has been washed away,' said the Mother to give her courage and consolation. The life of the woman was afterwards transformed.

Although many erring persons received a mother's love from her, her love would not give them the freedom to err. The slightest error in conduct would receive her notice. She might not always express it, but if it was needed, the delinquent was sure to get a reprimand from her. The sannyasin who developed pride because of his ochre robe, or the householder who showed scant courtesy to a monk because he was much younger in age, would equally get a warning from her about the dangers that lay ahead. If necessary she could be very stern too. If a person thought that taking shelter under her love, he could afford to do anything he liked, he was mistaken. Occasion would come when she would even order such a person to leave the place immediately. Of course, such occasions were very very rare.

A disciple might feel that her love was a sufficient guarantee against the ills of the present and the future life. But how much the Mother had to think for those whose responsibility she had taken! Even in her old age and even in her illness, she would be found to devote much time to prayer and meditation. When asked what was the necessity for her to do any spiritual practice, she would reply she was doing that on behalf of those who had taken refuge in her. No wonder if some disciples, after once getting her affection, felt no necessity of undergoing any spiritual practice at all. Did she not herself say,'If you touch water knowingly or unknowingly, are you not sure to get wet?' She herself once said to a woman disciple in reply to her question as to how she should look upon her, 'It is enough if you think of me even as your mother.' Sometimes her motherly heart could not bear that a disciple should undergo much physical suffering in practising hard tapasya. She would always warn the young aspirant against excess in such things. But at the same time she knew how to rouse to activity an indolent person who had imagined that spiritual progress was compatible with a life of ease.

Earlier, Saradamani's mother had felt sad that her daughter had been given in marriage to one who was half mad, as it were, and who did not lead a worldly life, so that her Sarada would not know what it was to be called 'mother' by her children. At this Sri Ramakrishna told her: 'Dear mother-in-law, you need not feel sorry. Your daughter will have so many children that she will afterwards be tired of being called mother.' His prophetic words came to be so true! We do not know whether the Holy Mother was ever tired of her children. But it is a fact that no mother under the sun had so many children as she had to address her as mother. And how great was their affection for her! A devotee actually said to her one day, 'You have got many sons like me, but I have got no mother like you.'

XI
LAST DAYS

After the passing of the Master, when the
Holy Mother would come to Calcutta, Swami
Yogananda was in attendance on her. His service
and devotion to her have become proverbial
amongst the members of the Ramakrishna Order.
After the death of Swami Yogananda, Swami
Saradananda took his place and looked to the
needs and comforts of the Mother. Among the
women disciples of the Master, Yogin-Ma and
Golap-Ma were especially devoted to her. When
she was in Calcutta they were her constant companions. They would often shield her against the
undue intrusion of people and sometimes against
the senseless display of devotion by sentimental
disciples which would cause her great suffering.

In the latter part of her life she often suffered
from malaria when she went to Jayrambati. On
such occasions Swami Saradananda himself
would go to Jayrambati or send physicians and
able hands to attend her. When she would return
to Calcutta she would look pale and emaciated, a
shadow of her normal self. But no amount of

suffering could cast any shadow on her spirit. She herself would say that her inner joy was never disturbed throughout her life.

In December 1919, she fell ill from fever. She was brought to Calcutta, but the fever continued to the anxiety of all. Even in her protracted illness she radiated wonderful peace, sweetness and light. She was considerate to all around her and was very careful that none should undergo much trouble in attending her. Sometimes she would behave just like a little girl, and sometimes she would talk in a high spiritual mood. Five days before her passing away, she said to a woman devotee who felt disconsolate at the prospect of her approaching end: 'Why do you fear? You have seen the Master. Just learn to make the whole world your own. No one is an alien. This whole world is your own.' This was her last spiritual utterance. She passed into Mahasamadhi at 1:30 a.m. on 21 July 1920.

The immortal spirit that had for the time being been clothed in mortal flesh was gone. But the example of the life of the Holy Mother lived and the message she left behind are potent means of transforming lives and a source of strength and inspiration to a large number of men and women. When one sees how her influence is spreading like the water of a flood-tide, one asks oneself whether she lived to continue the work of the

Master or to give added strength to his message, whether she was a disciple of Sri Ramakrishna or complementary to him. One wonders whether she was not an essential part of the same divine power that descended on earth to show light to the world and to guide humanity to the heaven of peace and bliss.

CULLED FROM STRAY TALKS

1. Everything depends upon one's mind. Nothing can be achieved without purity of mind. It is said, 'The aspirant might have received the grace of the guru, the Lord and his devotees; but he comes to grief without the grace of "one".' That 'one' is the mind. The mind of the aspirant must be gracious to him.

2. Don't puzzle the mind with too many inquiries. One finds it difficult to put one single thing into practice, but dares invite distraction by filling the mind with too many things.

3. It is essential to perform spiritual practices in a secluded place. When a plant is young, fencing is necessary, but when it grows big, the cattle cannot do it any harm. So after some years of meditation, when the mind is formed, you can remain anywhere and can associate with any type of person, and the mind will not be much affected.

4. Practise meditation, and by and by your mind will be so calm and fixed that you will find it difficult to keep it away from meditation.

5. Whenever the mind goes after anything other than God, consider that as transient and surrender the mind at the sacred feet of the Lord.

6. The less you become attached to the world, the more you will enjoy peace of mind.

7. Many turn toward God as a result of much suffering in life. But one whose mind is offered like a flower to the Lord right from childhood is indeed blessed.

8. The mind is no better than a wild elephant. It runs with the wind. Therefore one should always discriminate and strive hard for the realization of God.

9. One cannot escape the effect of one's past karma. But then, if a person leads a prayerful life, he gets off with only the prick of a thorn in the leg, whereas he was to suffer from a deep cut.

10. If you do not pray to God, what is that to him? It is only your misfortune.

11. When a man sees defects in others, his own mind first gets polluted. What does he gain by finding faults in others? He only hurts himself by that.

12. From desire this body comes into being. When there is no desire at all, the body falls away.

With complete cessation of desire there comes the final end.

13. As long as a man has desires there will be no end to his transmigration. It is the desire alone that make him take one body after another. Rebirth is inevitable so long as one has desires.

14. One must perform work. It is only through work that the bondage of work will be cut asunder and one will acquire a spirit of non-attachment. One should not be without work even for a moment.

15. Many are known to do great work under the stress of some strong emotion. But a man's true nature is known by the manner in which he does his insignificant daily tasks.

16. You should do work, no doubt. Work saves the mind from going astray. But then, prayer and meditation also are necessary. You must sit for meditation at least once in the morning and once in the evening. That will be like the helm to a boat. When one sits for meditation in the evening, there should be self-examination in respect of the works done in the course of the day.

17. Just as clouds are blown away by the wind, so the thirst for material pleasure will be driven away by the utterance of the Lord's name.

18. Even the water which has got a natural tendency to flow downwards, is drawn up to the sky by the sun's rays. In the same way, God's grace lifts up the mind which has got a tendency to run after sense objects.

19. The grace of God is the thing that is needful. One should pray for the grace of God. One must pray sitting on the bank of the river. One will be taken across in proper time.

20. The human teacher utters the mantra into the ear; but God breathes the spirit into the soul.

21. Just surrender yourself to Him; you will then feel His grace.

22. God-realization is just like a candy in the hand of a child. Some people beg the child to part with it. He does not care to give it to them. But without hesitation he hands it over to another whom he likes. All depends on the grace of God. He bestows his grace upon anyone he likes. Grace is the important thing.

23. God cannot be realized without love, yes, sincere love.

24. Have intense devotion to God. One must work hard. How can one achieve anything without effort? You must devote some time for prayer even in the midst of the busiest hour of the day.

25. To pray to God and meditate on him for two minutes even, with a fully concentrated mind, is better than doing so for long hours without it.

26. One's love of God depends entirely upon one's inner feeling. Love of God is the essential thing.

27. Give up this dry discussion, this hodge-podge of philosophy. Who has been able to know God by reasoning?

28. It does not become a woman to argue like that. Even the wise could hardly realize the nature of Brahman by argument. Is Brahman an object of discussion?

29. Neither mantra nor scripture is of any avail; bhakti or devotion alone accomplishes everything.

30. Lay the burden of your mind before Sri Ramakrishna. Tell him your sorrows with your tears. You will find that he will fill your hands with the desired object.

31. Even the impossible becomes possible through devotion.

32. Through these spiritual disciplines the ties of past karma are cut asunder. But the realization

of God cannot be achieved without ecstatic love for him.

33. Ordinary human love results in misery. Love for God brings blessedness.

34. It is idle to expect that dangers and difficulties will not come. They are bound to come. But for a devotee they will pass away under the feet like water.

35. What does a man become by realizing God? Does he grow two horns? No, what happens is , he develops discrimination between the real and the unreal, becomes conscious spiritually, and goes beyond life and death. God is realized in spirit. How else can one see God? Has God talked to anyone who is devoid of ecstatic fervour? One sees God in spiritual vision, talks to him, and establishes relationship with him in spirit.

36. Husband, son, body, or whatever it be, is all in maya. All these are maya's bondage. One cannot be freed unless one gets rid of bondage.

37. As you progress in your spiritual practice you will see the same Being in you as in me, and that He is in all men, be they of the lowest castes. Then you will acquire humility.

38. Can you call him a man who is devoid of compassion? He is a veritable beast.

39. In course of time one does not feel even the existence of God. After attaining enlightenment one sees that Gods and deities are all maya. Everything comes into existence in time and disappears in time. Gods and such things really disappear at the dawn of enlightenment. The aspirant then realizes that the Mother alone pervades the universe. All then become one.

40. Many may take the name of God after their minds have been hardened by the contaminating influence of the world. But he alone is blessed who can devote himself to God from very childhood.

41. Where is that competent student who can understand spiritual instruction? First of all one should be fit; otherwise the instructions prove futile.

42. One should be extremely careful about making His service perfectly flawless. But the truth is, God knows our foolishness, and therefore He forgives us.

43. Spiritual progress becomes easier if husband and wife agree in their view regarding spiritual practice.

44. All teachers are one. The same power of God works through them all.

45. Sri Ramakrishna never cherished any parochial or one-sided view. Brahman exists everywhere. The prophets and incarnations are born to show the way to benighted humanity. They give different instructions according to different temperaments. There are many ways to realize truth. Therefore, all these instructions have their value.

46. Do you know the significance of japa and other spiritual practices? By these the power of the sense-organs is subdued.

47. Past sins are counteracted by meditation, japa, and spiritual thought.

48. The mantra purifies the body. Man becomes pure by repeating the mantra of God.

49. From time immemorial so many people have practised image-worship and thereby got liberation. Do you mean to say that is nothing?

50. God is one's very own. One realizes him in proportion to the intensity of one's feeling for him.